AF415471

LHP

By Avis Turner

In The Land Where Fairies Cried Tears Of Stone: Grandma's Story

Moving to Bassett--Mama's Diary

Alzheimer's Disease Up Close

History Along The Smith River

LETTERS FROM A MARINE

Written by Elbert Conner Turner
August 1951 thru August 1953

Edited by Avis Turner

12-13-51

Turner Promoted In Marine Corps

PARRIS ISLAND, S. C.—Marine Private First Class Elbert C. Turner, son of Mr. and Mrs. Cecil Turner, Route 3, Bassett, Va., recently climaxed training here at the Marine Corps Recruit Depot by receiving a promotion to his

PFC. ELBERT C. TURNER

present rank. He also won the coveted silver cross of Marine Sharpshooter when he fired 212 of a possible 250 with the Garand rifle.

Turner finished training in field tactics, precision drill, military courtesy and Marine Corps history.

He fired other infantry weapons in addition to the Garand rifle and observed operation of the machine gun, mortar and flame thrower.

In Bassett Journal

Introduction

I knew I had the letters when we went through the home place and stored everything in our basement.

Just last spring my book was published about my husband and his battle with Alzheimer's disease.

I found these letters again in December 2018. I was fascinated with his telling about the two years in the Marines. He was drafted in 1950, called a year later. I knew him from church when we were growing up, but got reacquainted at a picnic in 1954, "orchestrated" by his mother and my aunt.

I thought the book about Alzheimer's could help others, caregivers, relatives, etc. These letters will tell who my husband really was.

Avis Turner – married to this marine for 56 years.

24 August 19 51

From: The Non-Commissioned Officer in Charge
To: Custodian of Records   Turner, Elbert Conner

Subj: Travel Orders

1. Having been Inducted this date into the U. S. Marine Corps, you will take charge of the below named Inductees and proceed this date as routed herein below to the city of Richmond, Virginia. Upon your arrival thereat you will report (with the Inductees in your charge) to the Officer in Charge, U. S. Marine Corps Recruiting Station, 323 East Grace Street, Richmond, Virginia.

1. Turner, Robert Hunter
2. Deering, Roosevelt
3. Jones, Jacob Donald
4. Thomas, Linwood Louis
5. Bane, Elvin Willis
6. Bane, Melvin William
7. Brandon, William Cosby
8.
9.
10.
11.
12.
13.
14.
15.

2. While performing the travel required by these orders you will conduct yourself in an orderly manner and you will be responsible for the action and decorum of the men in your charge. Any misconduct will result in Disciplinary Action.

3. The following necessary transportation request is furnished you herewith:

   T/R No. DA 86, 387 and 388
            (Transportation for   Eight   men)

4. The travel herein enjoined is necessary in the public service.

JAMES L. MOORE
NCOIC
SDRS
Roanoke, Virginia

Copy to:
OIC, DHRS, Richmond, Va.

I-T-I-N-E-R-A-R-Y

Depart Roanoke, Virginia   at   12:50 P. M.

Via   Norfolk and Western Railway

Arrive Richmond, Virginia   at   7:20 A. M.

Phone 82-8133 Richmond, at 8:00 A. M. tomorrow morning.

To: Mr. & Mrs. C. E. Turner, Route 3, Bassett, Virginia
Pvt. Elbert C. Turner 118074 – Plt. 392, Co. "C" –6th
Rec. Trng. Bn – Parris Island, SC
August 28, 1951
Dear Mother & Dad,

I finally got here Sunday 26th about 2 o'clock. Boy!
We really rode in "Style", by Pullman most all the way.

Everything is going fine, anyway what I know about it
is. They don't give us a history on anything, just what
they have to that will affect us.

We get up at 4 o'clock in the morning and go to bed at
10:00 o'clock at night. They have something for us to do
all the time, too. Keeping busy makes the day pass faster
though.

Our clothes were issued to us Monday and Robert T.
and I look quite different I assure you. All our work
clothes (which is all we have) are some color green. You
probably will have received my civilian clothes by the
time you receive this, they were sent home Monday.

Tell people hello.
Lots of love,
Elbert
From Parris Island, SC   6 cent Air Mail stamp,
postmarked Sept. 7, 1951
Saturday nite, Sept. 1
Dear Mom and Dad,

The best thing that has happened to me since I have
been here was to hear them call my name today at mail
call and to read your letter.

Boy, have we been busy! We used to think that I didn't get enough sleep when I was home, but here we hardly get 6 hours sleep. (in bed at 10:00 and up before 4:00). They have only been processing us this week—issuing our clothing, taking physicals, taking our measurements for our clothes, and so on. Our only trouble is that our actual training doesn't start until Tuesday, September 4 (by the way this is Sunday night now). So, it will be around October 31 before we get out of here. Seems like a long time, but it is only two months now. There is so much noise in here I can hardly think, maybe that will account for my mistakes.

I'll try to give you a run down of our activities here. Up at 4:00 make our sack, go shave, come back sweep out the tent and mop it, sweep the street and fallout for chow at 5:00. March to the mess hall and while we are marching we have to execute different commands. Eat chow in about a half an hour, fall out into rank and march back to the tents which are about a quarter of a mile each way and finish squaring them away if we didn't finish by five and if we didn't have them finished we get chewed out for it. Then we march to some other place for instructions and processing. Thursday, we had a classification test that lasted most all day. Out of a possible 150 score I made better than 120. There were about 30 of us that made it out of close to 140 men. Our time is certainly taken up to the minute of the 18 hours.

I guess you surely enjoyed your company this weekend.

Say, that lumber deal sounds like it might be alright if you can get two or three more haulers. When so you expect to get the planer.

Thanks a lot for sending Maxine's card on to me. She was supposed to send that before I left.

I hated to hear that Bobby had gone over and that Arnold Lee had been called, sure hope he gets a good deal. It won't be so bad if he does as told and in a willing manner.

Certainly was sorry I didn't get to see Duane before I left. Do you know if the hospital address is his present address or if it has changed?

I asked our Drill Instructor if we could have visitors and he said we could but we are restricted to the base and be only free until 10 p.m. Bobby's mother might like to come with you if you come and he wants you to bring him some stuff. Perhaps you can make it some Sunday. It certainly would be wonderful to see you, but it would be an awfully hard drive for you and would break both of you down. It might be better for you not to come, I don't know. You would have to decide that yourselves.

I'm terribly sorry that I haven't written before this but everything we do is on the march or run. There is no such thing as walking. But I haven't written to anyone else either so I'm not slighting you and I will try to write more often now that we are settled to a schedule and have started our training. I thought I would never finish this letter. All your letters have been coming through and they are wonderful.

I'll try to write a few lines tomorrow and I'll be seeing you around Oct. 30. By the way I am finishing this on Wed. the 6th.

With all my love,

Elbert

From Parris Island, SC – 6 cent Air Mail stamp.

Sept. 7, 1951

Dear Mom & Dad,

I have lost a day somewhere; I have been thinking all day that it was Thursday. We went to the Mess Hall at noon and I saw fish for lunch so I knew it was Friday. The chow here is much better than I expected, of course, it isn't seasoned very much, but we have plenty of it and usually they have a pretty good menu.

Wednesday, we took two shots, one in each arm, and my arms are as sore as if I had taken a lot of exercise. They are getting better though, thanks to the Drill Instructor's methods.

The Marines are alright now that we have gotten settled down. I think I would prefer the Marines to the army if I had another chance to decide even though we have to run all the time and have to take a lot of chewing out.

We had to wash clothes today and you would really be surprised to see how we wash them.

Bobby is taking it O.K. too. So I guess we have the Marine Corps under control. I would like to have you send me some cake or cookies, but we couldn't have but about one slice and they would take the rest or make me give the rest to the camp. We aren't allowed very much sweets, only what they give us at meal time so I guess you better not send anything and I don't know of anything I need now. I hope my clothes get there.

It's just about time for taps so I'll have to cut this off and I'll see you the first of November.

Lots of love,

Elbert

From Parris Island, SC

September 8, 1951
Dear Ma & Pa,

Here I am again tonight after a days work, and I do mean work. We have to put in a lot of work between now and next Saturday because we have review next week on the parade ground.

For supper today I went up for seconds and you know as usual when I eat too much my stomach hurts afterwards for awhile, but it has stopped now.

This afternoon for about two hours we played games on one of the fields (football and softball). We had a lot of fun and it seemed to make the whole platoon work better, and boy, after chow they really put us through the paces, too.

I haven't seen Kemp and I probably won't because he is in the air division and I guess they train in different places to what we do.

Well, it is about time to hit the sack so I'll be seeing you in a letter tomorrow I hope. Please tell everyone hello for me and that I'll write if I can get time.

Loads of love,
Elbert

From Parris Island, SC
September 19, 1951
Dear Mom and Dad,

How are you doing this beautiful Sunday afternoon? The sun is shining bright and there are a few white clouds floating around and we just got back from noon chow and had mail call. We had turkey and dressing, boiled potatoes, cauliflower, gravy, vegetable salad, two slices of bread with butter and <u>ICE CREAM</u>.

Boy, have we had it rough today. We got up at 5:00 this morning, cleaned up the area and moved out on the march to morning chow. Came back and I cleaned my rifle and bayonet and messed around until noon chow. Now we have nothing to do until supper. At 8:00 I go on guard duty until 10:00 tonight.

Whew, there is an argument in the next tent and it is hot and heavy. One of the guys was doing something he wasn't supposed to (lying on the sack) and he was called down by some of the others and being one of those guys who can't be corrected—an argument started.

I want to write Shep today and I'll close this one now, anyhow—there is no news. He wrote me the other day.

Tell people "Hi" from me.

With love,

Elbert

From Parris Island, SC

September 10, 1951

Hi Mom and Dad,

Here it is the closing of another day, or it will be in about three hours. It has been a long day, too. I got up at 3:15 this morning and we have been on the go since. Before breakfast we got out and did exercise and then double-timed for about a mile, came back, cleaned up the area, marched to chow and did it taste good. After chow we got our rifle and marched and drilled until about 11'o clock. I don't know how far it has been altogether, but it was enough. This afternoon we didn't have it too rough though, most of the time we were in classes and for an hour we didn't do anything but sit around and talk to the

D,I,'s about what to expect at the inspection that is coming up Saturday morning.

Getting back to the chow deal, we changed mess halls Sunday and the food is much better. Today at noon I made a jelly sandwich and brought it back with me and it sho' taste good (I'm eating it now). I'm going to eat some cookies and peaches now I brought back from supper. I'm eating three meals a day and am usually ready to eat each time, too. I don't know if I have gained any weight, but if this keeps up, I probably will.

Yesterday I wrote Pat and Shep, so I'll probably hear from them in a few days. I can't seem to find my address book, it may be in the coat I sent home—don't know. If I did will you please send me Duane's address or see someone and get it for me.

Well, I still have to clean my rifle so I'll be seeing you tomorrow I spect.

Loads O' Love,
Elbert

P.S. Tell Smitty and Carol to write me even if they don't hear from me for awhile because my time is limited.

From Parris Island, SC
September 11, 1951
Dear Mom and Dad,

This will have to be a shorty I guess because I only have ten minutes.

We had an exceptionally rough day today—on the go all day. They marched us across the island three or four times it seemed, and we didn't come in until after 7 o'clock tonight. After cleaning my weapons and taking a shower the time was almost gone.

One of the guys in our outfit fouled up today, so we have to get up at 3:30—another long day coming up. The whole platoon is angry at him. It will mean about an hour of exercise and running about a mile at double time.

I brought a ham sandwich back with me from the mess hall today and it was right on the spot. I just finished it. It is strictly against the orders to bring food out of the mess hall but it isn't what you do, it's what you get caught at, and besides they gave it to me and I just couldn't eat it all then.

I wrote to Maxine last night and aimed to write to Weaver tonight, but I just can't. They yelled lights out on me on the other page, but I'm writing by the street light. It is stretched across the street right by my tent luckily for me.

Well I speck I'd better hit the sack and try to get a few hours rest so I'll try to write tomorrow, maybe we will have more time to call our own if everyone clicks and doesn't try to get smart. If one person fouls up, we all catch the results instead of only the one who does it.
See ya,   Love in loads,
Elbert

From Parris Island, SC
September 12, 1951
Dear Mother and Dad,

Another day is nearing to end again and I'm tired. We got up around 3:15 this morning and been across the island two or three times today.

We had a field day tonight, that is, we had to move everything out of the tents and scrub the floor on our hands and knees with brushes then wash all the soap out and swab it dry with a mop. It was all very pleasant, though, because everything went smoothly. We had to double time for about a mile carrying our rifle before breakfast so I had quite an appetite. If I don't gain weight, it surely won't be because I'm not gaining on the amount I eat. I don't know how I do it, but I seem to eat more at each meal.

The lights just went out and the Corporal caught me and asked why I wasn't in the sack and if I wanted to stay up all night so I better quit. I'll try to write tomorrow.
Lots of Love,
Elbert

From Parris Island, S.C.
September 13, 1951
Dear Mom & Dad,

We had another full day today, didn't finish up and have mail call until after 10:00 tonight, so I'm sitting in bed writing with one eye and watching for the D.I. With the other. Some fellow in the next tent got some cookies and stuff so I'm eating while I write, too.

They gave us two more shots today, and it wasn't bad at all. My arms are a little sore, but not much. We got our clothes from the tailor today and that's why we are so late. They are all winter clothes and do they fit.

I wrote Mary Campbell this morning about 5:00 and at spots during the day.

Ouch, I'd better stop this until I can have some time during the day to write a letter, I almost got caught again.

I find out about if you can come at the time you said. We will be at the Rifle Range—I don't know.

Until tomorrow, goodnight.

All my love,

Elbert

P.S. Only got two more A.M. Stamps, close shave again.

Postcard from Parris Island, SC
September 18, 1951
Dear Mom & Pop,

I'm powerful indusris (sic) tonight, writing a letter and card in the same day, but I don"t think I asked you to send me some candy and cookies in the letter. Sho' would like to have a few bars of candy and a box of cookies if you can fix it up without too much trouble. Don't put chewing gum in it though because we can't have it. Maybe you can put in a half pound package of peanuts, too. We all like salty things because we sweat so much. I may be on the rifle range before it gets here, but I get mail there the same as here. I am mailing an air mail letter the same time as this card so see which gets there first and let me know. If the card gets there first, then I'll start using a 3 cent stamp instead of air mail. Be seeing you before long.

Love,

Elbert

From Parris Island, SC
Sept. 18, 1951
Dear Mom and Dad,

Here it is Tuesday of the next week and this is about the first breather I've had since Thursday night that I had any energy to write a letter.

It hasn't been especially hard, but we have been on the move continuesly (sic).

Friday night we had to get ready for the inspection which was called off because of rain. We got up at quarter to three Saturday and packed everything up and moved that afternoon and night. So, now instead of living in tents we are in quonsit—spelling? Huts, twenty-eight fellows in one and thirty-three in the other. Sunday, Bob and I went to Mass and came back and washed clothes. Then we had to police up the area for rocks, sticks, and paper, rack (rake?) it down and smooth out some paths to walk on. Oh, by the way, our Saturday inspection was rained out—wait I said that didn't I, That's what happens when you have to stop and do something for the D.I.

We were supposed to go to Elliot's beach today but it was rained out too. It seems that so far the rain has been in our favor maybe.

Say, you better start using dates on these Sundays and so on because I don't have a calendar to check the date on, but this coming Sunday is the 4th Sunday and I have to move again, this time for the rifle range on Saturday and it will take Sunday to square away. However, I asked the D.I. If we could have visitors while out there and he said yes, so the 5th Sunday or I believe it's on the 30th—you can come down if you want to so far as I know now. It will be a long tiresome trip for you though just to get to repeat it again in about 30 days if you plan to come for me when I graduate. Shep might come with you and help you drive if you want him to, I don't know. If you come be sure to bring some food, perhaps a plain cake and several candy bars of assorted kinds and some of that assorted life saver things because they last longer and can be eaten without observation. But don't put in any chewing gum for they take all of that.

I got a letter Sunday from Shep and one yesterday from the gang in the office. Shep's letter was signed by several people including Uncle Rupert Light.

The time is passing pretty rapidly now that we have started our schedule. It isn't as rough as I expected it to be so far, and I'm feeling fine now. In an hour and a half after I eat I'm hungry again and I'm hungry pretty nearly all the time. That's a darn good sign that I'm getting in pretty good shape, I think.

I'll try to write again tomorrow night so I'm going to try to write the office gang tonight after chow.
Heaps of love,
Elbert.

From Parris Island, SC
Sept. 24, 1951
Dear Mom & Dad,

I just got a few minutes to write so it's going to be short. I'm here at the range at last and had one days work out. We moved in Saturday and squared away Sunday.

Sept. 26, Wed. morn.5:20

We were all in a parade and inspection Saturday morning.

I got my cake Friday night and it was wonderful. It was what I had been wanting for several days. I think I got about 4 good slices so, I guess I ate my share of it. Yesterday I received the other box and it surely hit the spot.

Friday morning I went through the gas chamber and it was the first time apple blossoms ever made me cry, but we all had a lot of fun out of it.

They are keeping us pretty busy now and my letters aren't quite so frequent as they were. I have letters from Pat, Mary Campbell, Shep, Bud, and Claude that I haven't answered and I want to write Kemp and Duane too plus a few others. Perhaps I get more time after we settle down a little more. I think we start firing some of the weapons next week so that should be interesting.

Well, my time is about up so I'll put this in an envelope when I can.

Bob and I will be looking for you this weekend if nothing happens. If it does happen you can't make it we'll see you later I guess.
Heaps of love,
Elbert

P.S. I got a couple minutes. The Mess Hall out here isn't as nice as the one at the main site, but the chow is pretty good so I can't complain. Gotta go.

From Parris Island, SC
October 4, 1951
Dear Mom and Dad,

I have finally found an extra minute so I can write. We have been pretty busy this week running here and there and everywhere. We started firing Tuesday and it is qdite a lot of fun too. Yesterday I fired a score of 172 our of a possible 190 from 200, 300 and 500 yard lines. Today I made a 198 score from a possible 250 on the 200, 300 and 500 yard lines. I didn't do so well, today did I? Tomorrow I want to fire something over 200 if I can.

Hey, I saw Kemp on Monday!! We were in the same class tent but all we got a chance today was to signal to each other across the room over about 30 other guys heads. Sho' did want to talk to him, but didn't get a chance to. He looked fine though like the Marines work and was agreeing with him too. You can tell Joan I"m still trying for a chance to see him.

Gee, this week has gone by rapidly. I guess we are kept so busy that we don't have time to think. It surely makes us sleep good and eat enormously so it's bound to be good for us.

We got in with all the candy and peanuts Sunday and I gave out all the cake. The candy certainly was good, the only thing it just gave out to quick and we didn't give but a little of it away. When you send another box of candy put in mostly bars of different kind—it doesn't take so long to eat them as the lifesavers and we just grab a bar and run hide to eat it—figuartively speaking. If you like, just send a box of one kind will be fine and less trouble to make up.

Well, I just got a few more minutes and I still got to make my sack and take a shower by the time for taps.

Tell everyone hello for me, and tell Shep I'll write when I can, but he could still write another letter before I answer his last letter.

Be seeing you. Loads of love, Elbert

From Parris Island, SC—Pvt. Elbert C. Turner, Plt. 392 co. "C", 6th Rec.Trng.Bn.

Oct. 13, 1951

Dear Mom & Dad,

Please excuse the pencil, but my pen and paper are down in my sea bag so I'm using Bob's. We finally got together, he is in the bottom sack and I'm in the top. Boy, what a day!   We moved into the mess hall, but today and of all places, we are at the Women Marines Mess Hall down at the main side The chow here is twice better than what we have had though and all you can eat.

Well, we finished up at the Range with flying colors, everyone but one qualified in our Platoon. I made Sharp Shooter with a score of 212 points out of a possible 250. I had 39 in the offhand on the 200 yard line and 49 in setting rapid on the same line, 42 slow fire on 300 yard line, 45 rapid fire in the 300 yard line and 37 on the 500 yard line. (By the way, this is Tuesday night.) Bob made marksman with a score of 197.

We aren't supposed to say anything to the women, but occasionally we do. I think I've said eleven words to them since we've been here. I'm in the galary (sic) washing pots and pans and helping the cooks when I can. It is right hard work, but I don't mind it too much. The cooks are all nice people to work with, that is, they aren't all the time chewing us out and we don't have to be so formal with them. For supper tonight we had fried chicken and after we secured they gave us two huge trays of it. Must have been at least twenty chickens. I got into the milk locker and ice cream freezer, so you know what happened then—<u>um</u>. This mess hall is nice to work in, too; it is more like a cafeteria than anything else. We feed about 500 people each meal and in a very short time.

Well, I have some pretty important news this time. Just before we left the range I was interviewed by the Company Officer and offered the opportunity to go to O.C.S. when I come back from my leave. I haven't said I would take it yet though. It would mean about three years in here all told. I would go to school for about six months first and then serve active duty and still be in the reserve, but it would mean a lot more I think. I have about decided to take it if they offer it to me to decide if you think it would be advisable. You think it over and let me know what you think in case I have to tell them something before SI leave on liberty. To me, it sounds like a pretty good deal--2nd Lieutenant when I come out of school and a chance to make 1st Lt. Maybe by the time I get out of service.

I think I graduate on Monday morning the 29th and leave Tuesday morning about 8:00 or 9:00; so, it would mean you would have to come down Sunday and stay over until Tuesday. That might not work to well for you to be away that long, I don't know.

This is now Wednesday (couldn't spell it) morning. They gave us a half hour break, our first one.

Some of the guys want to know what route I take to get home, so of you will, write some of the major cities down for me. I would appreciate it.

Well, I guess this is enough for me now, so I'll to write again soon. Let me know what you think about O.C.S. for my future military career.

Oh, I saw Kemp at a concert the other night and we had a very nice chat.

Loads of love,
Elbert

Postcard of Atlantic Beach, N.C. Postmarked November 12, 1951
Dear Mom and Dad,

I got here OK and I have the car on the base. I don't have my permanent tags yet, but will get them this week. We had a holiday Sun. & Mon., so we have been to Atlantic Beach, Moorehead City and Newburn (spelling?). Not too much to do, but we have had right much fun riding around seeing the few sights. I don't know my complete return address yet, will let you know what it is.
Love, Elbert

From MCAS Cherry Point, N.C. Now Pfc. Elbert C. Turner, Hq.Sq.-11MAG-11
Postmarked U. S. Navy, Nov. 17, 1951, 3 cents stamp, Thomas Jefferson picture
November 16, 1951
Dear Mom & Dad,

Things are certainly different here on Cherry Point. We don't get up until 6 o'clock and go to work at 8:00, quit work at 4:30 and can go on liberty on or off the base after work every night if we don't have duty, if we want to. We can go to bed or sit on it anytime. Everyone has duty about every fourth night by sections. You don't do anything then usually. We can go to the show on that night if we want to but have to be back by 9:00 muster. The theater is on the base.

I had to work last night until about 8:00. By the way, I am in an office connected with Squadron 11 right at the hanger. I am in the operations division that is, it takes care of the flight schedules, route maping (sic), hour logging, and so forth. We are going to have to work all Saturday and Sunday this weekend (which doesn't happen very often).

I'm writing this while I'm sitting on my rack so please excuse this mess.

There are officers by the dozens coming into the office every day from Col's down. They are all pretty nice though.

I got my base tag Tuesday and didn't have a bit of trouble. They didn't even inspect the car.

I'm staying in a brick barricks (sic) and it is like a mansion compared to P.I. It actually has shades in the thing so you can imagine the comfort of it. We have a lounge room in the same building and coke and candy machines.

I think maybe I'll get to come home as I had planned unless something comes up which it always can, but as it stands now I think I'll make it.

Tell everyone hello for me and I'll be seeing you,
Loads O' love,
Elbert

PFC______________________________1186074
Hq. Sq. -11   MAG 11 Marine Corps Air Station
Cherry Point, N.C.
Pfc. Elbert C. Turner, Hq.Sq.11 Mag.-11 MCAS Cherry
Point, NC
November 27, 1951
Dear Mom & Dad,

I sho' miss that turkey dinner now, but those sandwiches were good for breakfast and lunch. I sacked in until 7:15 Monday morning. The trip went fine.   I drove to Smithfield in 3 hours and 40 minutes and was walking up to the barracks at 10:30. I picked up a Marine in Durham and brought him to Kinston where he turned off for Lejeune. It stopped raining on me about Raleigh and hadn't rained a bit when I got here.

Say, that cake is certainly good. We had some of it last night just before we hit the sack.

By the way, I drove to Smithfield on ten gallons of gas. That just about averages fifteen miles to the gallon.

Well, I have just about told all the news there is around here, so I'll try to have some more soon. Tell everyone hello and I'll be seeing you.

Loads of love,
Elbert

From Pfc. Elbert C. Turner
postmarked U/ S/ Navy, three one cent stamps
December 6, 1951
Dear Mom and Dad,

Cherry Point is still here, but nothing exciting is going on. I am getting plenty of work to do to keep me busy most of the time. I work through most of my lunch hour

now and send out for chow. Last weekend I worked
Saturday and Sunday. The work is pretty interesting
though and I am learning a little more all the time and am
being given a few more duties and responsibilities all the
time. They are talking about clearing me for confidential
data pretty soon now. I've been working setting up a new
filing system for the past two days, running errands,
taking the Colonel's wife home and so forth.

We had a parade Saturday morning, but by having to
work I got out of it—lucky me. Say, you should have
seen it though. Parade by the troops both men and
women and then the formations of airplanes flew over.

Boy, this Marine Corps certainly can get fouled up
especially in the pay department. I haven't been paid
anything yet. Something has got to be done about it,
'cause this old foolishness has got to come to a startling
<u>whoa.</u>

I have just about bought myself a suit of blues that are
about as good as new, in fact, they look fine, for $30.00
which is $35.00 less than a set from the store would cost.
They fit me perfectly, too. If you think it is alright to get
them, will you cash in my dimes and send me the $30.00
so I can pay for them, please. I don't want to spend the
money I have with me, for it would just about break me.
If you, do, Just fold the bills in a letter will be alright.

By the way, I thought you told me that my radio
wasn't fixed. One day last week one of the fellows
turned it on and it played as good as ever. It sho' did
surprise me.

Hey, I got your box and letter today at the same time
and it surely was good. I gave the Colonel and Captain
some and we just had a party. O man! That mug really

got the laughs when I held it up—ha ha haaaaaa. I wouldn't take anything for it now after the teasing.

I hope to get home for Christmas, I put in for it to start on the 24th of December and I think I will bet it because the Colonel signed it, so, I'll be seeing you then if nothing happens.

Well, I reckon I'll go take a shower, so, hold the fort down and tell everyone hello for me and take care. That lumber business seems to be doing OK with $700 loads going out.

All my love,

Elbert

Pfc. Elbert C. Turner Hq.Sq.-11Mag-11 MCAS, Cherry Point, NC

December 9, 1951

Dear Mom & Dad,

What a beautiful day it is and has been down here. It has been rather warm though, like an early summer's day. A slight breeze has been blowing in from the ocean most of the time making it very pleasant.

Well, as per usual I had to work again Saturday morning and had standby duty in the barracks this weekend, but have had nothing to do. This morning I polished my shoes and they look better than they ever have before.

Ummm---this candy sho' is good.

I pressed my pants this afternoon and it helped worlds. The jacket was too much to tackle on a locker box, though.

Howard and Frances are finally going to take the final step it seems. I received an announcement this week of

their coming marriage on the 22ⁿᵈ of December at 8:00
p.m., it must be formal, with a reception after the
ceremony at her home. I surely would like to go. That
just leaves me one more to marry off now, the one and
only--" Shep".

I wonder if you would make an appointment with
Wyatt Buick to have my car fixed while I'm home
Christmas, please.

One of the guys that sacked in close to me got married
Saturday at 4:00 and did we have fun teasing him for
about a week, but he has an apartment in New Bern now,
so he won't be sleeping in the barracks now except when
he has duty.

Well, that's all the Cherry Point news for now, so I'll be
seeing you soon I hope. Loads o' love, Elbert

Pfc. Elbert C. Turner, Hq.Sq-11, M.A.G. 11, M.C.A.S.
Cherry Point, N.C.
December 11, 1951
Dear Mom and Dad,

I am writing this at the office during my lunch hour
and I only have one sheet of stationery, so it won't be a
long mess. It has been raining here since last night and it
is about to get wet.

They are warming up the airplanes and it is quite
noisy around here. I haven't had too much work to do
this morning though, just enough to keep me comfortably
busy. I finally got around to writing to Duane and Bob
this week. It will probably be a surprise to them,
especially Duane.

I have been trying to decide whether to send any
Christmas Cards or not this time. We have been thinking

about going to New Bern Saturday afternoon after work so I might get some then. It would be nice if I could get some with the base as a subject. I
wouldn't have any trouble deciding which one to send where.

You haven't heard if Harry Dalton got married on his leave have you?

Say, I knew Anna Lee was married, but I never did think to tell you. No one much knew about it until it had already happened.

"Boots" are coming in here like mad. If this keeps up they will soon take over the base from the NCO's and Officers.

Well, I guess I had better see if I can find something to do so I can add up some points.

I'll be (Captain just walked in) seeing you soon.
Loads of love,
Elbert

Pfc. Elbert C. Turner, Hq.Sq.11 M.C.A.S. Cherry Point, N.C. Dec. 19. 1951
Dear Mom & Dad,

This card (enclosed) represents the six groups that comprises M.A.G.-11. All the operations work is compiled in our office.

Brrrr, it is chilly down here. Everyone goes around at a fast step now get from one place to the other out of the cold.

I got the money and have been trying to let you know that it arrived, but I never could get started on a letter. It's a good thing I didn't use my money because I didn't get paid again and it seems I won't for awhile too. I went to see about it and they don't even have my record. I'm pretty well broke now, but maybe they will come through the next time. It should be a right sizable sum, too.

Well, I have some more cards to address so I had better get at it. I'll be seeing you soon so hold everything down until then.
Heaps o' love,
Elbert

P.S. Thanks a lot for sending the money.

Postmarked U. S. Navy, Jan. 4, A.M. 1952
Thursday, Jan. 2, 1952
Dear Mom and Dad,

I got here alright Tuesday night at 12:30. We had fog almost all the way from Durham and part of the way from Danville. We stopped only once; to gas up in Kinston, and it took either 13 or 16 gallons of gas—I don't remember which, but I think it was 13. There wasn't too much traffic after we left Danville.

Wow! They surely put me back in the harness with a bang. We did almost as much in one day as we usually do in three. Tonight we had field day in the barracks from 6:30 until after 8.

It is beginning to get cool here tonight, but up until now we have had weather up to 70 degrees.

That chicken and cake came in handy the next morning for "brunch". I'm eating the last banana now.

I go to pick up my overcoat tomorrow; I might need it yet if it keeps getting colder.

Hawkins said 'thank you' for the jug. I had a big kick carrying it in like I had a jug of moonshine.

It is about time for lights out, so I write again soon.
Love,
Elbert

Postmark, U.S. Navy Jan. 9 a.m.1952
8 January 1952
Dear Mom & Dad,

It is still cold here and work is going along at a steped (sic) up pace so everything must be alright. I worked all day Saturday and Sunday and until 12:00 Monday night. I thought I was going to have to work tonight, but didn't finally.

Hey! It snowed ad sleeted down here Sunday evening about dark. There was just a little but it did snow. Cold enough to make you step right lively too.

Well, I have finally been cleared for confidential matter. They went back and checked all my records so they must be in order. Everything except my pay recod and I'm going to see about that tomorrow I think. The office is finally going to get behind me and see if we can get something done.

I still don't know just what the date is that we will ship out on. I'm kind of looking forward t it though. I like it here pretty well, but there we will have less guys so I think it will have its advantages. I believe it will be a few miles closer to home too.

It is about time for lights to go out so I'll write again another time. Tell everyone hello for me and hold the fort down and keep that lumber rolling in and out.
Love,
Elbert

Postmark, U. S. Navy Jan. 11 a.m. 1952
January 11, 1952
Dear Mom & Dad,

Here it is the end of another week of work and this has been quite a week. This is the fourth night of work. Last night I left the office at 20 minutes of 1. I didn't come in until about 9:00 this morning though and they have given me Saturday off after I muster at 7:45. I don't know what I'll do. Perhaps I'll go get a haircut sometime tomorrow. This is, I think, the last night of this midnight work.

Hey, I got the box in this mornings mail and the cake is all gone already. Everyone that got any of it thought it was great and that goes double for me. Joe said tell you it surely hit the spot.

At long last I think I am about to be paid. I told the Colonel about it and he did some telephoning then and again today. He said enough so that they got busy and found my pay card and I am to go to disbursing in the morning. I think they have had my card for some time just as I told you, but I'll probably never know for sure.

I surely hated to hear about Mr. Perdue. If you write to them please give them my best wishes for a quick recovery.

There is nothing exciting to write about so I'll try again another time.
Love,
Elbert

Postmark, Cherry Point, N.C. Feb. 1, 1952
January 31, 1952
Dear Mom & Dad,

Here is a short note at last. This is the first letter I have written since week before last, so I'm up to my old tricks again it seems.

Boy, all things in a turmoil here. We have been packed up since most of last week ready to move. I still don't know when we are going to move either.

That phone call Sunday night didn't cost but $1.25. It surely surprised me at being so little.

I got the box yesterday and it sho' was good. The cake didn't last very long, but I didn't show the rest of it so I had some left over. It is in my locker now. How did you know I waned some apples? I have been craving an apple for weeks; so, they surely hit the spot.

We had right much snow here Tuesday, but none of it stuck so we just had the beauty of it while falling.

I still don't know when I'll get to come home. This weekend I have duty and maybe we'll move next week so, maybe it won't be more than two or three weeks.

I'll try to write another short note soon so it won't be so long next time. Be sure and take it easy.
Loads of love,
Elbert

Postmark, U. S. Navy February 5, 1952
February 4, 1952
Dear Mom & Dad,

Here it is—that next short note. This is about my hardest task—writing letters that is. Still nothing exciting happening here. I received two letters in January, one dated the 17th and the other the 19th and haven't answered either of them yet.

Sgt. Hawkins had me out to his home for diner (sic) Sunday and did I eat. Really made a glutton of myself. It was wonderful to eat a home-cooked meal again though. After the dishes were cleaned up we went riding although it was pouring rain that didn't stop us. We went to Atlantic Beach and saw the ocean and watched the waves come in and were they big. You could see them from way out and start to roll up and the white caps ride along on the crest of them and when they hit the under current they would roll over like a ball of cotton rolling in the wind except there was a great roar with a tremendous splash as they hit the beach and washed up on it leaving it smooth as glass.

Tomorrow is payday again so I'll be coming into the chips again.

I still don't know the day we will be shipping out.

Joe said remember him to you.

Gotta o now for awhile.

Loads of love,

Elbert

Hq.Sq.-11, M.A.G.-11 A.L.F. Edenton, N.C.

February 14, 1952

Dear Mom & Dad,

Here I am back on the base and have put n a day of appearing to be working. I got into (sic.) Edenton at 9 o'clock last night and was in the barracks at 9:30. It wasn't to (sic.) heavily traveled until I left Oxford. The roads are pretty good most of the way, too.

Everyone was asking how I found things at home and were very sympathetic. Ed Odom, a Tech Sergeant recorded my leave time and only charged me with 4 days leave instead of five.

The base is going to be fine I think, very small so that makes it nice. We are having the Virginia weather here so you know what that is. The chow is much better here than it was at Cherry Point. It is prepared better and a better quality it seems.

I told them at the office today that I want to go home next weekend and I think maybe I will get it. Don't know yet for sure.

Note the change of address on the front of the envelope.

It is about time for lights out, so I will have to write more another time.

Be seeing you.

Love,

Elbert

No return address.

Thursday night, February 27, 1952

Dear Mom & Dad,

At last the inspections are over, but am I tired. We have really been working this week. The last two nights it has been from 12:00 to 2:00 before I got to bed and I got up at 5:30 this morning—three and one-half hours sleep. They didn't say one word to me though, so I must have been O.K.

I got to Edenton Sunday night about 10:30. It snowed on me the most of the way. From Roanoke Rapids it changed to rain on in. In Edenton I picked up a Marine and as it turned out he was a cook so we stopped at the

Mess Hall and he fried some ham and eggs for us. This was around eleven o'clock—it sho' did hit the spot.

My car is still giving me trouble so I plan to go into town Saturday and see if I can find a place to have it fixed.

We haven't been bothered by the flu here on the base at all so far as I know, a few colds now and then, but that is about all. I am fine except for one thing, my appetite seems to be boundless. I seem to starve before each meal come around. We had chicken today in honor of the inspection and I surely did justice to it. We also had mashed potatoes, green beans, broccoli, tomatoes, cole slaw, ice cream and another think or two. It was a real meal.

Tell Smitty and Carol to take it easy and get rid of the flu and their colds, and find out how little Joe is.

If you see Shep tell him I tried to get over to see him. You might ask Smitty to tell him too, as he will probably see him before you do.

It is about for lights to go out, so I write again another time. Take care of yourselves now.

Loads of love,

Elbert

No return address.

Mon. 3 March 1952

Dear Mom & Dad,

Another rainy day is about to come to a close down here. It started raining here yesterday evening and has been at it off and on ever since.

There isn't much going on here except a little work now and then.

I think I have found a place to have my car fixed. It is a General Motors garage and they handle Buick, Pontiac, Oldsmobile and Cadillac. Pretty good dealership I'd say. Anyway he has the market cornered on those cars.

What have they done about the Club Martinique? I hope it hasn't closed down, because it is a nice place to go for some quite (?) entertainment.

I hope everyone is getting over the flu and other sickness that they have been contacting. We still haven't been bothered to (sic) much by it here. I 'spect the regular routine helps combat it a lot.

There is no news to write so I'll try to write again soon. Take care and tell everyone hello for me, please. Heaps of love,
Elbert

Cpl. Elbert C. turner Hq.Sq.-11, MAG-11
A.L.F. Edenton, N.C.
March 19, 1952
Dear Mom & Dad,

It certainly is pretty here this morning, the rain stopped around 8:00 and the sun is shining on everything with a wonderfully fresh look. The birds are flying around singing so happily in the warm spring morning.

I am writing this while at work so you know I'm working awfully hard. The work comes in spurts, fast then slow—very boring at times.

I made pretty good time coming back Sunday night. I was in the barracks at a quarter to two, but I stopped at Smitty's and Danville, leaving Danville at twenty minutes to ten. I'm still having trouble with my generator. It charges then discharges, just sort of dances back and

forth. The speedometer cable seems to be having
something to do with it, so I'll properly (sic) will have
that fixed I 'spect.

I still have a slight cold but I am making it alright
though.

Hey, I got my pictures back this week and I had pretty
god luck with them, only one double exposure. The most
of them were taken down on the beach. It was a bright
sunny Saturday afternoon, and we had nothing to do.
The hike turned out to be a lot of fun though. There was
four of us, Joe Melillo, A. D. Robinson, Gerry Cody, and
myself. We tried to get some unusual shots, but didn't
have to (sic) much success at it. You can see how you
like them.

Gotta go now so I'll write more latter (sic). There
seems to be nothing new to write about anyway.
Loads of love,
Elbert

postmark: U. S. Navy p.m. MAR 24 1952 14008 BR – 3
cents stamp
Sunday, 23 March 1952
Dear Mom & Dad,

Here is another week ended and the start of another
leading us a little farther in our two year enlistment. I
hope parts of this next week won't be like parts of the
past one though. This is the first day out of the past four
that I have been out of bed to amount to anything. I have
no idea what it was unless it was the flu because I was
not sick at my stomach. I have a horrible cough and that
has/and is bothering me as much as anything, it made my
throat raw. I have been sitting up quite a bit today to

gain my strength back so I can go back to work tomorrow.

A letter from Aunt Lena came and I had a time trying to figure part of it, her writing is worse than it was when I was in school. I think I'll ask her for Phyllis Ann's address.

The way things look now I won't be home this weekend so don't look for me unless you here (sic) different.

It is about time for lights to go out, so I'll write again 'fore long.

Take care now.
Heaps of love,
Elbert

Cpl. Elbert C. Turner
Hq. Sq.-11 M.A.G.-11 A.L.F. Edenton, N.C.
Tuesday, 1 April 1952
Dear Mom and Dad,

Here it is at last, believe it or not. Everything is under control here, I reckon, at least there are no complaints worth voicing. The weather has been a little changeable, but that is to be expected. Some of the trees have started putting out right much and the grass is getting very green.

Say, that medacine (sic) was fine, but it got here to (sic) late for I had already gotten up and practically over the flu. One of the fellows that sleeps next to me got sick just as I got up so I gave it to him to take, but he was finally admitted to Sick Bay last night so I guess it didn't do him any good. The fellows certainly were good to me while I was sick though, they would go out and get stuff for me to eat and were all the time coming around and asking how I felt and if I wanted anything. Why, one of the guys even went into Edenton and got some oranges and lemons for me just because I said I would like to have some. The fruit seemed to help me as much as anything I had. Now, I'm feeling pretty near as spry as a spring chicken.

I got my car fixed except for a minor part that they didn't have, but it set me back a pretty penny—just $22.05. Perhaps I can get the part when I am home Easter. Yep, I think I can be home for the weekend, but I don't know if I will get Easter Monday yet or not. Anyway it will be good to get back for a weekend again though.

There isn't much news to write about so I guess I'll have to wait until something happens for me to write about. Besides, I'm sleepy, I had to stay up all last night as Duty N C O and I didn't get to sleep this morning as I was suppose (sic) to because a couple of our office personnel had to be out this morning. It isn't so bad though as long as I don't get still to (sic) long at a time. I'll get a half a day off later on for it though when it will work in with my plans better.

I'll be seeing you Easter I hope so take care and keep everything under control until then.
Loads of love,
Elbert

postmark: U. S. Navy, Apr. 6, 1952
Friday. 4 April, 1952
Dear Mom & Dad,

This is going to be a shortie 'cause it is 11:30 now. Anyway you will know I'm still kicking.

We had another inspection today in preparation for another big one around the 15th of April. I thought we were through for awhile.

I got the box today and it sho' was good. I am keeping it in the office to eat on it while I work.

Well, it looks like I'll get to come home next weekend (it will be next weekend when you get this). I can't understand why it takes so long for my letters to get to you when I get yours the next day after they are mailed. Even the boxes get here the next day. Your letters are postmarked from 2:30 to 5:30 and I get them the next afternoon almost every time. I think mine would get there almost as quick from all the way across the country as they do from here.

I suppose Smitty has gone to Roanoke and Carol home by now.

Gotta go now so I'll see you Easter I hope.
Love,
Elbert

postmark: U. S. Navy, Apr. 15, 1952
Monday, 14 April, 1952
Dear Mom & Dad,

Just a shortie to let you know Ralph and I got here alright. We left his house at eight last night and were at the barracks at 1:30. Everything went along smooth as silk. I hit rain one time that was so heavy it was hard to drive in, but it only lasted a few minutes. We stopped once for gas and that was all. The car did fine all the way so maybe they have it fixed now. I surely hope so.

I went to Sick Bay this morning and the report showed improvement, I guess. I'll be alright pretty soon. This is my spell for the year maybe. You know I usually have one every year or so.

There is nothing to tell except on myself and that is secret so I 'spect I better quit for now.

Be seeing you.
Heaps of love,
Elbert

postmark: U. S. Navy, May 6, 1952
May 5, 1962
Dear Mom and Dad,

Man O' Man what a beautiful day it is here. The sun is shining brightly without a cloud in the sky, The temperature is mild though, so it is just right to work. There is only one thing wrong though, I have to be inside and can't get out enough.

This past weekend was the third in a row that I have had to work and I'll be darned if they are going to get me the fourth unless something drastic comes up. Weekend before this last I had to work on an order for a parade and review for the 2nd of May. Today the Colonel put out a note "<u>well done</u>" so we feel right proud about it. I wasn't in the parade itself, but the order for it came from this office so naturally that's what made it successful.

We got another man in our office today so we have a job of breaking him in now but more to do the work.

I'm going out to Jack Detzel's house tonight He and his wife have invited the old gang out for a get together. It sounds like fun—huh?

Don't let me forget to bring my tax book back with me when I come back this weekend. The Lieutenant wants me to teach him some tax procedures.

Gotta go now so I'll be seeing you soon I hope.

By the way, how was the trip?

Heaps O' love,

Elbert

postmark: U. S. Navy, May 31, 1952

May 30, 1952

Dear Mom and Dad,

Here it is another month almost gone and I still don't feel like a Marine. I think they might as well give up trying to make me one, but they seem to be a most presistant (sic) lot.

Well, I'll try to give you a resume of what has been going on since I left home last time (darn, I can't write down what I think fast enough). We had no trouble coming back the other weekend, however, it did rain on us most of the way, but it kept some of the traffic off the road I think. It didn't take us too long—we drove it back to the base in about seven hours. That's around 320 miles. I got three or four hours sleep so I made it pretty well the next day.

The work hasn't been so hard just sturdy (steady?) and more of it than I have been able to get done, but by and by I'll whip it though.

Say, we had quite a display on Armed Forces day. I thought perhaps you might get a sudden idea to come down here to see it. The base was open to the public and we had a pretty good crowd of people most of the day from Edenton and outlying towns. The report from the people of Edenton was that it was the best ever had here and the Colonel had to give out with another "well done" to the personnel. We had a couple of flying boxcars, two or three jets, some prop driven fighters, a transport, a cabin plane, and some helicopters. The crash crew put on a good demonstration and we had several small layouts of other equipment. The spectators were quite impressed by the jet which put on an airshow and also by four prop-driven fighters which participated. We were handicapped though by the fuel restriction.

On Monday after A.F.D. Robbie started checking out so we didn't have any more help from him which meant that I had more duties along with everyone else. He was discharged Saturday last and Larry Hawkins (he is a second Lieutenant and nephew to Sergeant Hawkins in my office) and I took him to Suffolk to catch the train. After we got Robbie settled, Larry and I went to Virginia Beach for the rest of the evening. We walked up and down the Boardwalk just looking the place over for future use in case we wanted to use it. There wasn't much going on, but it was a change from the regular routine, It was three o'clock Sunday morning before we got back to the base What? No, I didn't go to Williamsburg at all. I called Carollyn from Edenton and she was going to be away for the weekend (worse luck), but like always I managed to have a pretty good time.

Sunday morning I got up in time to go in to Edenton and went to church. I thought it might be an opportunity to meet some people and it seems it might be a pretty good idea too, if I can follow it up. Everyone was very friendly but as a whole all the people are very friendly and treat us as human beings. That afternoon I rode around town and took in a movie. A very quite (sic) and restful day I think.

Monday when I went to work, I went in as Assistant Non-Commisioned Officer in Charge to Sergeant Hawkins, so I'm coming up in this man's outfit. It means more responsibility though in quite a few ways. In fact it meant—for one thing—that this weekend I had to stay here on call the whole weekend, while everyone else in the office except Captain Meyer shoved off Thursday night for a long weekend liberty. Oh well, I don't mind though, I don't have a pocket full of money anyway. Payday isn't until Monday week either; so It looks like I am going to have to borrow some money so I can get home this coming weekend, to. I don't know though. Ralph and his wife are coming home with me, so I don't reckon I will have any expense which means I might get by without borrowing any after all.

Jack and Bev are still planning to come home with me, too, so put the little pot in the big one, but don't go to very much trouble. I know it will mean some extra work for you both, but it isn't necessary to do so much.

Yesterday morning (Thursday) we went on a troop hike down the beach and back around the road. I guess we made a round trip of six to eight miles part of which was through the boondocks. We all had quite a time of it. It was much different from boot training and everyone got a big kick out of it.

By the way, Thursday afternoon the Bloodmobile was in Edenton and I went and donated a pint and while I was there one of the registars (sic) got to talking to me and found out where I was from and as it turned out one of her friends in Edenton married a boy from Martinsville,

Harry L. Turner, Jr. She called her up while I was there so I'm to call on them next week sometime when I give them a ring. I don't know if his father was sheriff of Henry County or just ran for the office. It seems that I remember a Harry L. Turner ran for office four years ago this last election against Morton. I'm going to give them a ring though the next time I go into town I think.

Did you ever find out anything about Eanes? Dees ask me if I had any luck and I told him you were still trying for me.

I suppose you are tired reading this stuff by now so I'll come to a screeching halt and let you rest.

Tell everyone hello for me and I'll be seeing you.
Loads and loads of love,
Elbert

Sgt. Elbert C. Turner
Hq.Sq.-11 M.A.G.A.L.F., Edenton, N.C.
24 June 1952
Dear Mom and Dad,

I thought I might surprise you and write a letter for a change, that is, if you won't be too surprised.

We had a very nice trip coming back Sunday night. It was around 11:30 when we got back to Edenton. The mercury kept climbing the further this way we came and it has really been warm yesterday and today.

Nothing very exciting has been happening here that I can write about except that we have been working fairly regularly. I haven't done any night work yet, but have worked late in the evening, today that is.

Oh! We got a new boss Monday. Lieutenant Colonel no less. I don't know what kind of guy he is going to be, but we'll square him away if he isn't just what we want. This breaking in of new officers is getting to be old stuff now We only have one Lt. Col., three Captains and one 1st Lt. in our office now. I should certainly be indoctrinated into the ways of an officer by the time I finish my tour of duty.

I want to have a hay ride on Saturday night when I come home for the fourth if I can. If Glen S. is going to be home, he is supposed to plan it and have everything ready when I get home except the truck. I am going to write to him a letter and tell him to go ahead and plan on it.

Well there is no news so I'll just quit for this time.

Take it easy tand tell everyone "hi" for me.

Be seeing you the 4th.

Heaps of love, Elbert

Elbert on the right—I don't know the name
of the other marine, nor where they were.

TCL/tcl
16-3/4
31 Dec 1956

From: Director
To: SSGT ELBERT C TURNER 1186074 MCR
      RT. 3, BOX 115,   (7)
      BASSETT, VA.
                         AVU   7041

Subj: Transfer of Class III Aviation Personnel to the
       Marine Air Reserve Training Command

Ref: (a) MCO 1300.13

1. Reference (a) directs that the records of all aviation
personnel be transferred to the Marine Air Reserve Training Command. Accordingly, your records have been transferred this date.

2. In the future, address all official correspondence and
change of address to: Commander, Marine Air Reserve Training, Naval Air Station, Glenview, Illinois.

                              W. C. JAECK
                              By direction

16/E-1:rwr
23 Aug 1959

Mr. Elbert C. TURNER
Route 3, Box 115
Bassett, Virginia

Dear Mr. TURNER

    Your expiration of obligated service has terminated with the United States Marine Corps Reserve. Enclosed is your honorable discharge.

    Please note that your discharge certificate shows your rank as ________ Sergeant ______ pay grade (E-5). The new rank structure became effective 1 January 1959, under the authority of Marine Corps Order Number 1223.1. Under this new rank structure your pay grade was not reduced, however your rank was redesignated. Current regulations now prohibit making entries on the reverse side and a single red line drawn diagonally from the upper left to the lower right, will be made.

    I want to thank you for your association with the Marine Corps Reserve and if at any time we can be of any assistance to you, please feel free to write.

    Wishing you success in years to come, I remain

M. G. SHRYOCK
Captain, United States Marine Corps
Assistant Officer in Charge, Class III Records Section

postmark: U. S. Navy July 28, 1952
27 July 1952
Dear Mom and Dad,

The Ecenton Chronicle is about to go to press. The what for, wherefore, and general news is about to be put out for the subscribers of this paper to read.

The goings on here are not of a phonominal (sic) nature but here is what there is of it.

The base went on a seven day nine hour a day work week this past week. I don't know what they are trying to prove unless that it is awfully hard to get up at five o'clock in the morning. We are, however, finding enough to keep us quite busy during the day though. I had the duty this weekend and there was enough to do. It isn't so bad on weekends though because we all have right much fun while we are working. Today I cut the stencils and the Captains ran them off on the mimiograph (sic) machine.

Everyone pitched in and helped on everything. There were only four of us, as the rest had the weekend off, so the two Captains, Fred Sauer, the boy you met in the restaurant, and myself had the office to ourselves. Except for Hawkins, I am the only typist we have and "Hawk" doesn't do much of it. For the past five or six days I have been more or less glued to the typewriter. Getting a lot of experience. This weekend was all very informal, so it made for very nice working conditions.

Say, the Commandant of the Marine Corps is going to be here Friday, naturally this calls for a parade. You should be here if you want to see a bunch of sharp looking Marines. There is a catch though, my office has

to get the order out calling for the parade so typewriter
here I come.

Wow! This sounds like all work and no play, but
actually we have a lot of diversions, what with the
swimming pool, softball, boating, tennis, movies, and
several other things.

Hey, those lots you bought at the dam sounds great! I
am anxious to see them. It appears you were wise to
forget about the school property though at those figures.
I don't think it is worth that much to us. The property
ajoining (sic) would be of more value to us I think.

It seems everyone around there is getting married.
Poor people, they don't know what they're missing 'cause
two surely can't live as cheaply as one and besides there
is that very probable situation where an added expense
comes along.

By the way, what did C. L. and Jeff have to say about
my accident?

I have a favor to ask of you if it won't be too much
trouble. I would like you to either call or go in to see
Bob Atkins and see if he can get me a set of
garberdines(sic). That will include the pants, shirt, cap,
belt and tie. I can get them in Portsmouth for about
twenty dollars so you might check the prices if you
contact him or either see him. They look much sharper
than our regular issue uniform.

I went down to the Squadron office this past week to
try to get a leave the first week in August, but so far I
haven't had any luck. I don't know whether I will be able
to get it or not so don't look for me until you see me. If
and when I do get some time I may not be able to let you

know anyway so don't look for me until you see me. There it is— straight scoop.

I have not been able to locate my car title anyplace.

Well folks there is the news from Edenton and vicinity and as you can tell by the afore-printed news why this paper does not receive such a large circulation. I'll bring this stuff to a halt.

I'll be seeing you and tell everyone hello for me please.

Love always,

Elbert

Sgt. Elbert C. Turner

Hq. Sq. - 11, MAG -11 A.L.F., Edenton, N.C.

5 August 1952

Dear Mom and Dad,

Another week is well on its way now. They surely are slipping by with a rapidness that is amazing.

Say, that phone call was quite a surprise! It was great to hear from you although I could hardly understand you. We have one good line and one bad one and I think we got the bad one that time. I know most of the fellows on the switchboard and when I call out they always give me the good one if it is open. Of course the Edenton operator gave us the bad connection.

Everything is going along here the same as usual—a little work, a little play, and lots and lots of rumors that mean nothing. We know no more now than when last I saw you.

All the men are anxious to find out something, but someone can surely keep a secret. They are as tight mouthed as a mule is stubborn.

By the way, I can get four days leave the 15, 16, 17 and 18th of August or I can wait until the first week in September and <u>maybe</u> get six or seven days. It might be taking a chance to wait until September. Whichever you had rather, I can do. In September for six days leave, I can get nine and in August for four days I can get five. I'll leave it up to you what I do except I have put in a request for September which I think I could change if you want. September would mean more time and if I took that, then there would be no point in your coming down here for me the 16th and 17th because the month is about over then anyway and you could just wait until that time to come for me.

Well, they say 'nuff of anything is enough and this seems to be 'nuff of this foolishness so I'll be seeing you. Love always,
Elbert

postmark U. S. Navy Aug. 28, 1952
27 August 1952
Dear Mom and Dad,

Things are moving along rather quietly this week. Nothing very exciting ever happens here it seems, just the regular old routine stuff. Everything seems to be the same as when I left it except that we got in some new planes both jets and prop driven.

Oh, the inspection I mentioned that I had to get ready was held Monday afternoon. It was really a farce though. I think it took me about five minutes to lay it out and less time for them to inspect it. That's the kind of inspection I like. Surely wish they were all like it.

We went on a hike today but it wasn't exciting—to (sic) <u>darned far</u>. At 7:30 we started out and hiked all the way to Edenton in a round about way and back again by way of the road. It was only about a three and a half hour walk at a pretty rapid pace though. I think I'll be able to sleep without too much trouble tonight especially since it is raining.

It is 'most time for lights out so I'll see you later. Please tell everyone hello for me.

Loads of love,

Elbert

Sgt. Elbert C. Turner
HQ.SQ.-11. M.A.G.-11 A.L.F., Edenton, N.C.
7 September 1952
Dear Mom and Dad,

Well here we are back on station E-long! C-long! T-long! Again. The same old daily soap operas are on but we'll give you a rundown on them anyway—purely for refresher purposes of course.

The planes are still flying with no unusual occurrences. It seems that everyone has gotten the flying fever all of a sudden, because we just can't keep enough aircraft up to satisfy the pilots. Some of the pilots didn't get in the required hours last year and they don't aim for that to happen again I think.

We had another hurricane scare this weekend, but thank goodness the thing went back out to sea although it caused me to lose almost two nights of sleep. I got to sack in late one morning, so it wasn't so bad after all.

Oh! Oh! A parade is scheduled for Wednesday morning. I can't understand why I get myself into these things! We put out the order calling for these things is what makes it so bad. It looks like I could accidentally, but conviently (sic) lose the darned things; but no, they go right on through and then everyone is giving me dirty looks. Heck, this stuff is good for young Marines as my Captain would say. Anyway, I'm not complaining any because I usually have a good deal out of everything.

I've been carrying a book around with me for about four days and I haven't read but two chapters yet. I'm gonna sneak up on it one of these nights.

Hey! I went to Norfolk Friday evening on the Beechcraft and I saw _some_ Cruisers, Aircraft carriers, and a couple of Battleships. Of course, it was from the air, but they were beautiful boats.

Gotta sign off now so I'll be seeing you.
All my love,
Elbert

postmark U. S. Navy Sep 11, 1952
10 September 1952
Dear Mom and Dad,

We have heat in the barracks tonight! When they give us heat you know it's getting pretty chilly around here. It makes you step around right lively in the morning when you get up, mind you, I said when you get up and it 'sho is a hard task, too.

Well, what do you think? We had that parade today and I didn't have to stand it. That makes three in a row I have gotten out of. My luck can't hold out much longer, though I'm afraid.

I went to the dentist Tuesday and had my teeth fixed. Believe it or not, I only had one and that was one the filling had come out of so I had them to clean them while they were at it. My teeth surely look white and clean now. Feel good too.

I think I'm going to quit smoking cause they said that would stain your teeth and it isn't worth it.

We are getting a new guy in our office (a buck sergeant) so maybe he will be able to do some of the work. He can type which is just what we need to take some of the load off me.

It is about time for lights to go out again, so I'll have to cut this garble off now. This is a shortie, but maybe I can do better next time.

Oh, will you find out if Pat has moved yet and send me the new address if she has! Sho' would appreciate it.

See you later.

All my love to you,

Elbert

postmark U. S. Navy Oct 1, 1952

30 September 1952

Dear Mom and Dad,

This will be a shortie because there is absolutely nothing to write about. It has been a week and a half since I got back and nothing has happened to write about that is of any interest—the same old routine stuff all the time. I almost wish sometimes that something would happen to break the monotony of it.

But then I guess I wouldn't want it to change either.

Well, how are things going back there anyway? Probably the same for you—work a lot, eat and sleep a little. Better stop so much of that work 'cause it will make you tired. There is just no percentage in it. I'm allergic to such foolishness as you know.

Yes, the car is doing fine. I had no trouble coming back at all and I checked my gas mileage and found that I got around twenty miles to the gallon so that isn't bad at all if it will just maintain that average.

This is it, I just can't think of anything worth writing about.

Tell everyone "hi" for me and I'll be seeing you.
All my love,
Elbert

postmark U.S. Navy Oct. 15, 1952
14 October 1952
Dear Mom and Dad,

This is one day late, but at that it is some earlier than it was last time

We got back Sunday night at a quarter to one; so, it wasn't bad after all. There were some fog patches after we left Suffolk that slowed us down some. The old flivver did pretty good all the way back, no trouble at all. That heater would drive you out if it was turned on full force I believe.

There is still nothing doing here as per usual. The usual routine of work each day— in at 8:00 and out at 4:30 to mess around until 8:00 the next morning. Really, it's exciting if you like a rut.

Gotta go take a shower now, so I'll see you.
Loads of love,
Elbert

Sgt. Elbert C. Turner
Hq.Sq.-11, M.A.G.-11 A.L.F. Edenton, N.C.
28 October 1952
Dear Mom and Dad,

I'm a day late again with my letter, but everything is fine with us here.

Well we got here at 2:30 so we had time for a little sleep before we went to work. I didn't go to chow because we didn't eat any of that you packed for us, so I just sacked in and ate that. It was much better than what they had here.

The work has been fairly heavy so far this week, especially today as I had the office to myself most of the day. It had me hopping around pretty lively I must say.

Hey! I had something to work out just like I wanted it to. The Duty NCO roster came out and of all the good luck, I got it on the 4th of November. Man-0-man, I'll listen to the election returns all night Couldn't ask for a better deal than that could you?

Page said "Hello". He is a character that sleeps right next to me. He's another Rebel too from South Carolina.

When I come home the weekend of the 7th and 8th, I will have a Buddy with me. He, Billy Leazer, is a college graduate and majored in music. He can play a piano that will make you sit up and listen. Billy came in about the same time as I did and is a Buck Sergeant in the S.S. (selective service) bracket.

That is about all there is to write about so I'll be seeing you again later.
Love always,
Elbert

Going to a dance in Roanoke

with college friends, November, 1955.

postmark blurred, 3 cents stamp
Monday 24 November 1952
Dear Mom and Dad,

This is going to be a shortie. I have to go to the field tomorrow for a 48 hour watch. Should be a lot of fun though.

We got back without mishap It only took us 5 hours and 15 minutes to drive back to Edenton and we didn't drive too fast either. "Church" drove part of the way back and it surely helped out because he took over when I begain (sic) to get tired.

I won't get any leave Christmas but maybe I'll get a little time New Years, I don't know for sure yet. If I do get some time New Years it will be about five days and Church will come home with me.

Gotta go now.
Loads of Love,
Elbert
P.S. I will write another note later after my watch.
Postmark blurred, 3 cents stamp
14 December 1952
Dear Mom and Dad,

This will just be a shortie because there is nothing at all to write about as usual.

Everything is going along very smoothly and the same old routine—make out a few reports, do a little typing, answer the telephone, and run errands for the officers. It keeps us fairly busy all day though, and that is what we want, so at best we accomplish our aim.

The drive back Friday night was uneventful. I got into the sack at 1:30 so I don't know just how long it took me to make the trip.

I'm having to stand the Duty NCO tonight and my radio has been on all night. Sho' has been some good music on too. No, I haven't gotten the dial cord fixed yet; I am tuning it with my finger. The radio shop will fix it for me when I take the the cord.

Well, that's all there is for now. But I'll write again soon.
Love,
Elbert

Postmarked December 23, 1953
22 Dec. 1952
Dear Mom & Dad,

We just got these cards today. I'm only sending a couple of these, because I know this will be late and my others maybe.

I got the box today and declared today the 25th in order to open the large package and it is all gone now, too. The two smaller ones I haven't opened yet---I don't know.

The Colonel and his wife have invited me out for Christmas dinner at their home. I'm really looking forward to it.

Be seeing you,
My love to you,
Elbert
(the card was a drawing of Santa and two airplanes and "Season Greetings and Marine Aircraft Group Eleven")

Christmas card, postmarked December 23, 1952 with note:
Dear Mom & Dad,

Things are running very smoothly and in the usual
pattern. This Sunday morning seems very much the
same as any other morning. I guess the reason is because
I have to be in the office, whether we work or not.
"Hawk" went on leave last Wednesday so I'll have the
duty until the 28th when he returns, then I'll leave he 30th.
Please tell everyone "hi" and Merry Christmas for me.
All my love,
Elbert

Postmarked U. S. Navy Jan. 9, 1952
January 6, 1953
5 January 1953
Dear Mom & Dad,
    The first letter of the year. Wonder how many more
of these will be?
    We got back last night without mishap. It was no
strain at all. I got a fairly good nights sleep too except I
woke up about 6:30.
    Howard left this morning for Cherry Point for two
days school; so, for him it was pack, unpack and pack
again.
    We have a parade the 16th of this month. You know
what that means for me—work.
    That's all there is going on around here. I'll try again
later.
All my love,
Elbert

Sgt. Elbert C. Turner
Hq.Sq-11. MAG-11
A.L.F., Edenton, N.C.

0115, 6 February 1953
Dear Mom and Dad,

I have Duty NCO tonight. Actually I'm standing by for Joe so he could ship for home tonight instead of Friday night. My regular duty night will be the 21st of this month or Saturday week.

We got back Sunday night without mishap and didn't see an accident anywhere along the way. It turned out to be a beautiful night for driving and it certainly felt good to be driving a Buick back. The trip wasn't nearly so tiresome and I was in the sack by (or rather before) 2 o' clock.

Today was pay day as you will have decided when you opened this letter. They tried a new system on us, too. Our C.O. Put the money in individual envelopes and brought it around to us personally instead of us having to go to him. They are all the time getting new ideas of some kind.

Say, how does the "fliver" run now since they have worked on it? You said in your letter that it almost ran out from under you on the way to Roanoke Monday. If they got it fixed right, a good tune up job and so forth I'll bet it really does run now.

We have been working pretty steadily this week. There has been very very little extra time on our hands. The week has certainly gone by fast, hardly enough time to get done what I wanted and needed to get completed.

This picture was made at the CPX we had back in November I think it was. The other boy with me is Roger Bohl who is a Sergeant in my office. We were just getting ready to secure from the exercise when someone said let them get our picture so this is the results.

Well, that's all that has been happening here this week so I'll be seeing you. Please let me know if you get this letter with the enclosures. Bye now.
All my love,
Elbert

postmarked U. S. Navy Feb. 17, 1953
16 February 1953
Dear Mom and Dad,

Another trip completed safely even though we saw two accidents on the way back.
We saw the first out of Oxford—nothing serious, but it banged the automobile up some. The other one was just out of Roanoke Rapids and it looked like it might have been a serious one.

We stopped five times and I was still in bed before one o'clock. Darn it, I was still awake at two o'clock and when I did sleep it was for short naps.

Howard just came in (I'm writing this at the office after the movie of course) and said to tell you hello and that he is felling (sic) fine, but still hasn't gotten on the scales— he's afraid to. Ha.

Everyone excepting myself is getting ready for the inspection Friday. They have a preliminary tomorrow and Wednesday so you can imagine the sembelance (sic) of order around the barracks. That is why I'm writing at the office tonight.

Daggone, I can't spell worth fifty cents tonight.

Joe Melillo just walked in smoking a cigar just like John D. Rockerfellow (sic). He's going to call his girlfriend, by the way, he became engaged Christmas.

Here's something that might interest you. I counted up today and found that our Squadron is made up with a percentage of sixty-six and two thirds college graduates or men who have been to college and with a very few exceptions all are draftees.

This is all there is—there just doesn't seem to be any more news.

Be seeing you,
All my love,
Elbert

postmark U. S. Navy, Mar. 23, 1953
March 22, 1953
Dear Mom and Dad,

I'm just going to be able to dash off a few lines—what with packing and so forth.

I've been kept quite busy this past week and it seems that things are going to be rather crowded the next two weeks also. I learned today that I probably won't get back until about the 3rd or fourth of April.

We had a good trip back last Sunday although the rain made it a little hazardous. About sixty miles from Edenton we saw a deer on the side of the road. It was just getting ready to leap into the underbrush it looked like. That was the first one I have ever seen like that and as large as that one was. It looked like about a year old doe.

I told you those pictures turned out good. Even the one the flash didn't go off and is distingushable. (sic) The ones I took of the houses were all clear too.

Oh, I'm not going to take my car with me. The government is going to pay my expenses "by doggies". I think it will be wiser to leave it here anyway not knowing what provisions are being made for individual cars

Gotta be going now. I'll write again before to (sic) long. Take it easy and tell everyone hello.

All my love,
Elbert

postmark U. S. Navy, Mar. 30, 1953
March 27, 1953
Dear Mom and Dad,

Here it is the end of another week and it seems it just started. Of course it might be because I have, ah----been sort of busy most of the time.

I flew down to the Point Monday morning and started work immediately. The first thing was setting up sleeping facilities (which we got very little chance to use, but it was enough for the most of us). It was a little chilly, but there are very few colds and none of them bad—Marines are rough, ready and hearty souls don't you think. The food was excellent and believe you me, the meals never came to (sic) soon. Hungry all the time. Thursday we all moved back to main side and are now billeted in barracks. They certainly are hot and stuffy after the wide open spaces out on the sound.

Hey, I saw Mrs. Reeder today and she told me to call the Colonel and she would send us a cake while we are here. Think I'll take here (sic) up on it too, since they are here at the Point and shouldn't be too much trouble for either of them.

I haven't had a shower or change of cloths (sic) since Sunday and only two shaves— one Tuesday night with an electric razor and one with my gear this morning. I'm not cruddy or anything so horrible as that, but since I don't have to stay on duty tonight, I think I shall go to the barracks find a rack make it up go take a shower (if I' not afraid of the water) and hit the sack and sleep in a bed between sheets no less for a change. It has all been rather interesting and right much fun since it is a simulated war.

Better go now and get that shower now so tell everyone hello for me and be seeing you.

My love to you,

Elbert

postmark Edenton, April 16, 2 p.m. 1953, N.C
A Birthday Message for Mother – (she was born April 17, 1913) To the Dearest Mother Anywhere
Dear Mother:

Just a little note   Especially to say "You're loved a lot

and wished a lot of happiness today!"   HAPPY

BIRTHDAY he wrote: May this day be one of your

happiest and may you have many, many more. Love,

Elbert
A letter will follow soon,
"Bert"

postmark U. S. Navy, Apr. 17, 1953
16 April 1953
Dear Mom and Dad,

Another month over half gone again already. Time seems to be flying by at supersonic speed. Perhaps it is because I am busy most of the time that helps it go so fast.

Thank you so much for the box on the 15th It got here in fine shape in the morning and the cake was gone almost in less time than it took me to open the package. Everyone admired my shirt and sweater and what do you think they were saying. They were either wishing they were smaller or larger one so they could wear them. I wore them both that night to show them off.
Note: Elbert was born April 15, 1930.

We are having a parade Thursday the 23rd if everything goes according to plan. The General is to be here for this one, so it should be pretty big. My luck is still holding— I'm not to be in this one either as it stands now. I'm beginning to wonder if I could still march if something came up and I had to. Might be rather embarrassing if I couldn't.

Yes, you can tell Smitty and Carol to come down the weekend of the 25th and 26th because we plan to come home that weekend if nothing happens. Nothing better not happen is all I gotta say about it. We are, however, working on an order for another maneuver, but I have it finished before the weekend comes along. Tell Smitty and Carol I'll be looking for them on that weekend.

Oh, I got my license plates in the Tuesday mail and put them on Wednesday afternoon (the last day). It's a fairly easy number to remember too. Of course I've gotten kind of use to remembering numbers. That always helps.

Well, that seems to be all there is to write about so I'll let you rest up until the next one. Take it easy and we'll be seeing you soon I hope.

All my love,

Elbert

Sgt. Elbert C/ Turner

Hq. Sq-11, MAG-11 ALF, Edenton, N.C.

11 May 1953

Dear Mom and Dad,

Well, you're probably back from your trip by now and glad it's over too. I hope you had a good time and enjoyed your trip and visit with all your friends.

There isn't much doing here it's practically the same old thing with very little deviation from routine stuff. The weather, however, is beautiful now and makes me want to be outside instead of at a desk. If possible I'm going to be getting outside some too.

I received the bonds alright the next day after you mailed them and thanks a lot for sending them.

The boys came back from the maneuvers none the less for it, in fact, they all seemed to have had a good time anyway they had many tales to tell. I think the sand fleas gave them quite a bit of trouble.

Dawg-gone there is absolutely nothing to wright (sic) about and I'm about asleep now too.

By the way, here is the car payment as you can see.

We will be home in about a week from the time you receive this letter if nothing happens. There is one more weekend to struggle through yet.

Well heck I'll try again later maybe I can think of
something to say next time.

Be seeing you.

All my love,

Elbert

postmark U.S. Navy, May 27, 1953
UNITED STATES MARINE CORPS
Marine Corps Air Station Edenton, N. C.
26 May 1953
Dear Mom and Dad,

Here I am back at the base again getting back into
swing after a very relaxing weekend. I can't say it's the
same old routine though because I am going to start
going to work at 3 o'clock in the morning tomorrow. It is
to give us day-night training. We get off at noon though,
so we have the whole afternoon to do as we please.
Perhaps I can get a sun tan now.

We got back without trouble last night, I did find
however that I was missed, but nothing was said as it
turned out that I was off legally anyway. If I hadn't been,
it could have been rough.

The chicken came in handy today for lunch as I went
to morning chow. Yes, I got up at a quarter to seven and
was at work before eight I don't think I'll be shoving off
early any more—that was too close for comfort. It isn't
worth it with the time I have left.

Well, this is all the latest scoope (sic) so I better go
get some shut eye.

Love to you,

Elbert

In June 1961, Elbert Turner began a new job at People's Life Insurance. He worked for Stanley Furniture for twenty-five years. After retiring, Elbert worked for five years delivering flowers for a local florist until Alzheimer's made that impossible.

S Sgt. Elbert C. Turner

Hq Sq – 11, MAG – 11 A.L.F, Edenton, N.C.

21 July 1953

Dear Mom and Dad,

This will be a surprise I'll bet.

We got back at 5 o'clock and without any trouble. It was quite a warm trip though and today has really been a dilly.

Howard turned in at Sick Bay right after we got back and they kept him over there. I went over to see him this afternoon and he said they might keep him for a week. His cold is better though. They found that his blood is low so that accounts for his being tired all the time. Well, whatta you know! I expect to be transferred to the home base, Cherry Point, any time now. My orders are apt to come in any day now. Darn it, I guess it is about time some of the bad caught up with me. That means I probably won't be at Edenton when you take your vacation and that I won't be home anymore until I get out because they will not give out passes for more than 24 hours. Oh well, it won't for very long perhaps.

Things as a whole are fairly quiet around here. Everything is going along as usual with no one getting excited about it, just a few disgusted remarks.

That seems to be about everything so I'll be seeing you in August.

All my love,

Elbert

T/Sgt. H. L. Churchward 476601 Mag-11, M.C.A.s.
Edenton, N.C.
Addressed to Mr. & Mrs. C. E. Turner, Route #3, Bassett,
Virginia
July 22, 1953
Dear Folks-

Hi you all. Hope everything is fine with yawl.
Things are fine here except for my being in the hospital.
I had an examination as soon as "Bert" and I received our
visit with Edenton with a flourish of heat & foul odors.
At 6 o'clock Monday nite I was in bed in Sick Bay. I'm
getting filled up with a lot of different pills & medicines.
My blood pressure is way low & my chest shows dark
shadows of irritation due to my cold. I'm feeling a little
better today tho—all I've done is eat, sleep and take pills.

We sure had a nice hot trip back here—the ole steam
was just pouring off of us. I was sure glad to get back
tho—cause I was pretty ill.

Oh-Oh!! there goes the crash siren—wonder who hit
the deck now. Hope it isn't too serious.

The rumors are sure flying around here. I hope it's
just rumors, too—I'm not too anxious to go over seas
right now. Not till November or December anyhow.

The enclosed clippings are from Cherry Point's paper
& thought you might be interested in them. The one
about release applies to SSGT E. C. Turner. He shore
doesn't like the idea of it either—can't say as I blame
him.

"Bert" was visiting me last nite for a couple of hours
until I got too tired. I'm about due for a nap now and
some more medicine.

Hawkins orders for Korean duty were cancelled to make it possible for him to go with the Mag. Sure am glad—he is a nice guy to have around.

Before I close I'd like to thank you for everything this past week end. I just hope I didn't leave my cold with any of you.

Don't eat too much ole dead chicken & banana pudding. Bye now
Sincerely, Howard C.

11 August 1953
Dear Mom and Dad,

Here I am at Cherry Point as of 3 o'clock today. So, this is my last step in the Marine Corps on active duty for a while anyway. It is certainly a set up of confusion. No one knows what is going on. It took Joe and I about 2 hours to get things straightened out so I'd know what to expect. The barracks are quite crowded, but one can stand most-anything for 12 days. I guess having the room in the Staff Barracks spoiled me—no one else seems to notice it. Anyway, it is going to be a lot of rack time and doing nothing. I suppose I will get in some letter writing and reading.

There really is nothing to write about or if there is I can't think of any of it to write.

Gee. I'm sorry you couldn't take your vacation, but perhaps you'll enjoy a Florida trip better as you have been talking about one for so long. I'll be home then and perhaps take (care) of things for you so you can take a month. Long enough to really enjoy it.

I'll give you my new address now so I won't have to be chasing after my letter like I

have had to for the last week and a half.
Casual Company, Bks. 224 M.W.S.G. - 27
 MCAS, Cherry Point, N. C.
Be seeing you soon,
All my love,
Elbert
P.S. I almost wrote "Bert" instead of my right name.

S Sgt. Elbert C. Turner
Casual Company, Bks 224
M.W.S.G. - 27
MC.A.S. Cherry Point, N.C.
(in with the last letter)

Hi, again. I didn't have an envelope last night so I went to the P.O. Today and bought some.

Oh, I start tomorrow on my separation routine. I can't tell you just what it is going to involve.

By the way, would you call the Bank and ask them if I can wait until I get home to make my car payment. I won't get paid until I get our--ran out of ink--(was blue, now green) so I would like to keep what I have because I'm afraid I might need it. If they don't want to wait, then if you would give it to them I will repay you when I get home. Please let me know what you do?

Tell everyone "hello" for me.
Love,
El-"Bert"

Avis Turner was born in her grandmother's house in Bassett, Virginia. Her family was among the first residents of Collinsville in the 1940s. She graduated from Fieldale High School in 1952 and received a two-year Secretarial Certificate from Radford College in 1954. She has taken classes in creative writing at Patrick Henry Community College and independent study courses on writing and genealogy. Avis Turner has worked as a secretary, library aide, and bookmobile librarian. She published The Carter Family Tree in 1984. Her articles have been published in magazines and books including Grit, Women's Household, Virginia Microfilm News, Patrick County Heritage Books, and the Henry County Virginia Heritage Book. This is her fifth book. Her first *In The Land Where Fairies Cried Tears of Stone* detailed her grandmother's life in the Fairy Stone Park Area of

Patrick and Henry Counties in Virginia. Her second book

Moving To Bassett--Mama's Diary is about her mother

and growing up in Bassett, Virginia. Her third book

History Along The Smith River tells about the history she

grew up with along the river.

Our 50th Wedding Anniversary – August 24, 2007.

Moving to Bassett -- Mama's Diary

Avis Turner

HISTORY ALONG THE SMITH RIVER

AVIS TURNER

In The Land Where Fairies Cried Tears Of Stone

Grandma's Story

AVIS TURNER

BASSETT VIRGINIA
THOMAS D. PERRY

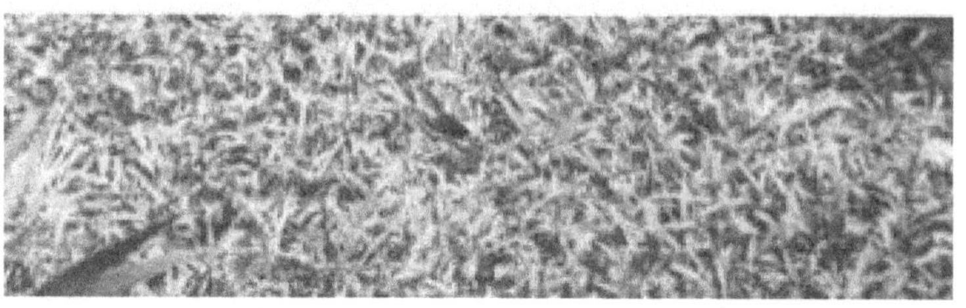

Avis Turner is also the "Cover Girl" in Tom Perry's photo history book *Bassett, Virginia*, shown above, at age four in her sandbox.

ISBN: 9798649611442
Copyright 2020 Avis Turner

This book was published via agreement with
Tom Perry's Laurel Hill Publishing

Thomas D. "Tom" Perry
4443 Ararat Highway
P O Box 11
Ararat VA 24053

276-692-5300
laurelhillpub@gmail.com

https://squareup.com/store/
laurel-hill-publishing-llc

Autographed copies available at https://
squareup.com/store/laurel-hill-publishing-llc
and
Available Tom Perry's Author Page on
Amazon at https://www.amazon.com/-/e/
B002F4UJGEA

www.ingramcontent.com/pod-product-compliance
Lightning Source LLC
Chambersburg PA
CBHW070817170726
48000CB00018B/1016